DEEP-SEA ANGLERFISH
AND OTHER FEARSOME FISH

Rachel Lynette

Chicago, Illinois

www.heinemannraintree.com
Visit our website to find out more information about Heinemann-Raintree books.

To order:
☎ Phone 888-454-2279
▣ Visit www.heinemannraintree.com to browse our catalog and order online.

©2012 Raintree
an imprint of Capstone Global Library, LLC
Chicago, Illinois

Edited by Megan Cotugno and Abby Colich
Designed by Philippa Jenkins
Picture research by Hannah Taylor
Originated by Capstone Global Library
Printed and bound in China by CTPS

15 14 13 12 11
10 9 8 7 6 5 4 3 2 1

Library of Congress Cataloging-in-Publication Data
Lynette, Rachel.
  Deep-sea anglerfish and other fearsome fish / Rachel Lynette.—1st ed.
    p. cm.—(Creatures of the deep)
  Includes bibliographical references and index.
  ISBN 978-1-4109-4195-4 (hc)—ISBN 978-1-4109-4202-9 (pb) 1. Oneirodidae—Juvenile literature. 2. Anglerfishes—Juvenile literature. I. Title.
  QL638.O5L96 2012
  597'.62—dc22   2010038187

Acknowledgments
We would like to thank the following for permission to reproduce photographs:

Caters News Agency Ltd p. 20; Corbis p. 28 (Julie Dermansky); FLPA pp. 10, 13 middle, 18, 22, 23, 24 (Minden Pictures/Norbert Wu), 26 (S Jonasson); Image Quest Marine pp. 12 top, 12 bottom, 13 bottom, 14; naturepl.com pp. 4, 7, 9, 13 top (David Shale), 6 (Solvin Zankl); NOAA pp. 25, 21 (ALASKA FISHERIES SCIENCE CENTER); Photolibrary pp. 11 (Peter Arnold/Darlyne A Murawski), 16 (Peter Arnold/Jonathan Bird), 17 (Peter Arnold/Fred Bruemmer), 27 (Peter Arnold/Jeffrey L. Rotman); Photoshot p. 15; Science Photo Library p. 8 (Martin Shields); SeaPics.com p. 19 (David Wrobel); shutterstock p. 29 (©Pixel1962)

Cover photograph of deep-sea female anglerfish (*Melanocoetus*) reproduced with permission of naturepl.com (David Shale).

We would like to thank Michael Bright for his invaluable help in the preparation of this book.

CONTENTS

Some words are printed in bold, **like this**. You can find out what they mean by looking in the glossary.

DEVILS OF THE DEEP

Deep-sea anglerfish are small fish with huge mouths. They look so scary that they have earned the nickname "seadevils."

Fishing poles

One important way anglerfish are different from other kinds of fish is that they have their own fishing poles! An anglerfish has a **ray** called an **illicium** attached to its snout. At the end of the ray is a fleshy bulb called an **esca**, or lure. The esca is **bioluminescent**, which means it glows. The esca glows because of a special kind of bioluminescent **bacteria** that lives inside of it.

The esca on this anglerfish glows because there are bioluminescent bacteria living inside.

Deep-sea anglerfish live where there is little to no light.

Ocean Zones

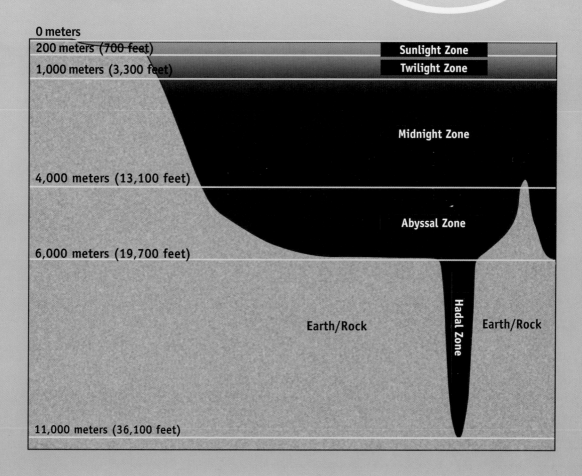

0 meters
200 meters (700 feet) — Sunlight Zone
1,000 meters (3,300 feet) — Twilight Zone

Midnight Zone

4,000 meters (13,100 feet)

Abyssal Zone

6,000 meters (19,700 feet)

Earth/Rock   Hadal Zone   Earth/Rock

11,000 meters (36,100 feet)

Deep in the Ocean

There are more than 160 **species** of deep-sea anglerfish. They can be found in almost every ocean of the world. They live deep in the ocean where there is no sunlight and it is very cold. Deep-sea anglerfish live up to 4,000 meters (13,123 feet) below the surface, in the midnight zone.

TEETH, TEETH, AND MORE TEETH

If you saw a deep-sea anglerfish in the wild, the first thing you would probably notice is its teeth. Deep-sea anglerfish have large mouths that are filled with many long, sharp teeth. The teeth are curved inward to keep **prey** from escaping. Some deep-sea anglerfish even have teeth outside their mouths!

An anglerfish's mouth is full of long, needle-like teeth.

The anglerfish's body

Most deep-sea anglerfish have round bodies. They do not have scales. Instead, they have thin, blotchy skin. Some deep-sea anglerfish have bumps or spikes. They can be black, gray, or brown.

Mini monsters

Deep-sea anglerfish look terrifying, but they are not so scary once you realize how small they are. Most **species** of deep-sea anglerfish never grow beyond 13 centimeters (5 inches) in length. That is small enough to fit inside a teacup! However, a few species do grow bigger and can reach lengths of up to 102 centimeters (40 inches).

Most deep-sea anglerfish are small enough to fit inside a teacup.

13 centimeters (5 inches)

TIME TO EAT

Deep-sea anglerfish cannot afford to be picky eaters, because there is not much to eat deep in the ocean. They will eat anything they can catch, from small fish and squid to shellfish. Deep-sea anglerfish have **elastic** throats and stomachs. This allows them to eat animals up to twice their own size!

Lure them in

Without sunlight, the body of the deep-sea anglerfish cannot be seen in the deep water. However, its glowing lure can be seen. The deep-sea anglerfish keeps its body still, but moves the lure in front of its mouth to attract **prey**. Once a fish or other prey comes close enough, it is sucked into the deep-sea anglerfish's giant mouth.

Helping Each Other

The **bioluminescent bacteria** in the anglerfish's lure help the anglerfish by attracting prey. The anglerfish helps the bacteria by supplying it with food. When different species help each other, it is called symbiosis.

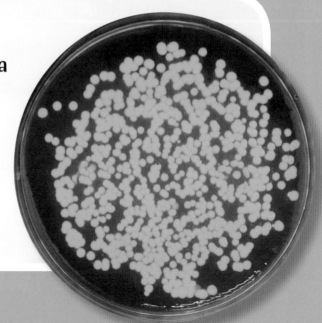

A deep-sea anglerfish uses its glowing lure to attract prey.

BIZARRE BREEDING

So far, all of the deep-sea anglerfish you have been reading about in this book have been female! Male deep-sea anglerfish are different from the females in many ways. Males look different and are much smaller.

Attached for life

When a male reaches adulthood, it cannot feed itself. In order to survive, it must find a female and attach itself to her body with its teeth. In some species, its body fuses with the female, becoming part of her.

This male deep-sea anglerfish is starting to fuse with the much larger female.

In these species, the **internal organs** of the male start to deteriorate, or break down and disappear, until the male is completely dependent on the female. When the female lays her eggs, what is left of the male is there to **fertilize** them.

A single female has been known to host up to six males.

Where Are the Males?

At first, scientists were puzzled at finding only female deep-sea anglerfish. They also wondered about the **parasites** that seemed to be attached to most of them. Eventually they realized that the parasites were actually the males of the **species**.

DEEP-SEA ANGLERFISH ROLL CALL

Football fish

The football fish is thought to be the first deep-sea anglerfish ever seen by humans when one washed ashore in Greenland in 1833. Bigger than most deep-sea anglerfish, it can grow up to 46 centimeters (18 inches).

Black seadevil

The large mouth of the black sea devil is wider than its body when it is open. Its gel-like body helps it to survive in deep water.

Fanfin anglerfish

This **species** has many long, thin **rays** that extend from its fins, tail, and body.

Whipnose angler

This species of deep-sea anglerfish has a longer lure than any other species. It can even be longer than the body of the fish!

Leftvent

This fish has a large **barbel** dangling from its chin. The barbel looks like seaweed and helps the leftvent to lure **prey** to its mouth.

THE VICIOUS VIPERFISH

In addition to deep-sea anglerfish, there are many other interesting and frightening deep-sea fish. One of these is the viperfish. Unlike most anglerfish, the viperfish is long and thin like an eel. It is about 30 centimeters (1 foot) long and has glowing spots on its belly called photophores. The photophores are used to attract **prey**.

The glowing spots on this viperfish are called photophores.

A viperfish's teeth are so large that they stick out of its mouth.

Many teeth

Like the anglerfish, the viperfish has many long, needle-like teeth. A viperfish's teeth are so large that they do not fit in its mouth. Instead, the bottom teeth curve upwards in front of the viperfish's eyes.

Migrating fish

Although viperfish live very deep in the ocean—up to 5,000 meters (16,400 feet)—they **migrate** closer to the surface at night to find food. Viperfish are fierce hunters. It is thought that a viperfish hunts by lunging toward its prey and stabbing it with its long fangs. They eat mostly small fish such as lanternfish, mackerel, and anchovies, as well as shrimp and squid.

THE WOLFFISH

Wolffish live deep in the Atlantic Ocean. They can reach up to 1.5 meters (5 feet) in length. They spend most of their time in nooks and small caves.

New teeth each year

A wolffish has four to six large teeth that stick out of its mouth. It also has three sets of crushing teeth on the roof of its mouth. The wolffish's teeth are perfect for crushing its **prey**. They eat anything with a shell that they can find, including crabs, **mollusks**, and shellfish. Chomping on hard shells wears their teeth away fast. Luckily, wolffish grow a new set of teeth each year! While the new teeth are growing, wolffish do not eat anything at all.

This wolffish is bigger than you!

Without wolffish, there would be too many sea urchins.

Where Are All the Wolffish?

Wolffish numbers are dwindling due to overfishing. By eating green crabs and **sea urchins**, wolffish keep these **populations** under control. Scientists worry that these populations will grow too large if there are not enough wolffish.

THE FRIGHTENING FANGTOOTH FISH

Fangtooth fish live very deep in the ocean where the water is nearly freezing. Although they look quite frightening, fangtooth fish are only about 15 centimeters (6 inches) long. Fangtooth fish have prickly scales and are brown or black. They have small eyes and poor eyesight. Fangtooth fish hunt by swimming around in the dark water until they bump into something they can eat, such as another fish or squid. Fangtooth fish may be eaten by larger fish such as marlins or tuna.

This fangtooth fish is small enough to fit in a cereal bowl.

Fangtooth fish are named for their long, sharp teeth.

Big teeth

For the size of its body, the fangtooth has bigger teeth than any other fish in the ocean. In fact, the largest two teeth on the fangtooth's bottom jaw are so big that the fish has actually evolved to have holes in the roof of its mouth. When a fangtooth shuts its mouth, these two gigantic teeth slip into the holes instead of stabbing the fish in the roof of the mouth.

THE BLOBFISH

Blobfish live deep in the ocean near southern Australia. They are rarely seen by humans in their natural **habitat**. The body of a blobfish is about 30 centimeters (1 foot) long. It is filled with a gel-like substance that is slightly lighter than water. This allows it to float just above the seafloor without swimming. Blobfish spend most of their time floating, waiting for food to come to them. They eat **sea urchins**, **mollusks**, and shellfish.

Blobfish have soft, flabby bodies.

Many eggs

Blobfish lay thousands of eggs at a time. They tend to float over their eggs. Scientists don't know if they do this to protect the eggs or just because they are too lazy to move away from them.

Caught by accident

Blobfish frequently end up in nets that were meant for lobsters and crabs. Because they cannot survive for long out of water, they almost always die in the nets. Humans cannot eat blobfish, so these fish die needlessly.

These dead blobfish were caught accidentally.

LIFE IN THE DEEP

It can be tough to survive deep down in the ocean. The lack of sunlight means that it is completely dark. There is not much oxygen in deep-sea water. The water is very cold. There is also a great deal of **pressure** from the water above. Imagine having a bucket of water on your head. Being thousands of feet down in the ocean is like having thousands of buckets of water over your entire body.

There is no light deep in the ocean.

Red dye has been used to show the bones and **cartilage** of this anglerfish.

Animals that live in deep water are **adapted** to this environment. A fish that has adapted to deep water would expand, or even explode if it were brought up to the surface.

Tiny Bones

Deep-sea anglerfish have very tiny, soft bones in every part of their bodies. Having a light body allows them to swim in deep water without being crushed by the pressure.

EXPLORING DEEP WATERS

Most of the deep waters of the oceans have been left unexplored. Deep water covers a large part of Earth. Some scientists believe there may be thousands of yet undiscovered animals living in the deep.

Remotely operated vehicles

Today much of the underwater exploration is done using vessels that are specially made to withstand the **pressure** of deep sea. They are usually unmanned and are controlled **remotely** by people on a ship. They are armed with cameras and robotic arms. One of the most important of these **submersible** vehicles is the *Ventana*. It has been in operation since 1988. It has made over 3,000 trips into deep waters.

The *Ventana* must be lowered into the water by a crane.

Autonomous Underwater Vehicles

Autonomous underwater vehicles are also used to explore the deep sea. Unlike remotely operated vehicles, these vehicles are smaller and do not need to be tethered, or attached, to a ship. Rather than being controlled remotely, they are programed to perform specific tasks.

Autonomous vehicles are smaller than remotely operated vehicles.

TOO MUCH FISHING

Deep-sea anglerfish are too small for humans to eat. But they often get caught in fishing nets. Deep-sea **trawlers** drag nets with heavy weights along the ocean floor. The dragging nets destroy fragile deep-water **habitats** and the nets capture whatever gets in the way. Fish that are **adapted** to deep water cannot survive the trip to the surface. Biologists fear that some **species** may be destroyed before they are even identified.

Trawlers, such as this ship, damage deep-sea habitats by dragging nets along the ocean floor.

Several species of deep-sea fish have been caught in this net.

Important fish

Deep water anglerfish, as well as other deep water fish, are important to the ocean food chain. They are a source of food for other, larger fish. They also eat smaller animals, so that the **populations** of those species do not grow too large.

Too Few Babies

It takes many years for most deep-water fish to reach the age where they can breed. This means that trawlers may be killing fish before they can **reproduce**.

DEEP SEA IN DANGER

In April 2010, an **oil rig** exploded causing a deep-sea oil well to leak huge amounts of oil into the Gulf of Mexico. Fish and other deep-sea animals cannot live in an oily environment. Even fish that are not directly exposed to the oil could die from starvation if the smaller animals they eat end up in the spill. Scientists fear the spill will cause serious damage to the underwater environment.

Millions of fish have been killed by the oil spill in the Gulf of Mexico.

Air pollution contributes to global warming.

Global warming

Even where there is no oil spill, the deep sea is in danger. **Global warming** can harm the deep sea. Global warming can cause the temperature of the ocean to change. It can also cause less food to grow and less oxygen to reach deep-sea waters. Deep-sea anglerfish and other deep-sea fish may not be able to survive these changes. These fish are an important part of the food chain. We need to protect deep-sea fish by taking better care of our world.

GLOSSARY

abyss very deep area of the ocean

adapt to adjust to conditions in the environment

bacteria single-celled, microscopic organisms

barbel feeler on the jaws or lips of some kinds of fish

bioluminescent light made by living organisms

cartilage elastic connective tissue found in various parts of the body, such as the joints

elastic able to stretch and then return to its original shape

esca fleshy bulb that acts as a lure

evolve change slowly over time

fertilize begin reproduction

global warming raising of Earth's temperature. Global warming is caused by increased amounts of certain gases in the air.

habitat place where a plant or animal lives

illicium fishing rod-like ray that is attached to the head of an anglerfish

internal organs parts of the body that are inside, such as the heart, liver, and kidneys

migrate move from one place to another

mollusk animal with a soft, unsegmented body, usually with a shell

oil rig platform and equipment used for drilling oil

parasite organism that lives on or in another organism, usually causing it harm

population group of organisms of the same species that live in a particular area

pressure force pressed on something

prey animal that is caught and eaten by another animal

ray slender rod extending from the body or fins of some types of fish

remotely operating something from a distance

reproduce to have babies

sea urchin small, soft-bodied animal that is enclosed in a round, spiny shell

species group of animals or plants that are similar and can reproduce

submersible able to go under water

trawler fishing boat that pulls large nets through the water

FIND OUT MORE

Books

Cerullo, Mary, M. *The Truth about Dangerous Sea Creatures*. San Francisco: Chronicle Books, 2008.

Coldiron, Deborah. *Anglerfish (Underwater World)*. Edina, Minn.: Buddy Books, 2007.

Pipe, Jim. *Scary Creatures of the Deep*. New York: Franklin Watts, 2009.

Websites

http://animals.nationalgeographic.com/animals/fish/anglerfish.html
Read more about the anglerfish at this National Geographic site.

www.seasky.org/deep-sea/anglerfish.html
Visit this page to discover more information about anglerfish.

www2.scholastic.com/browse/article.jsp?id=3748096
This site provides information on submersibles. There is also a slide show of amazing deep-sea creatures.

www.mbari.org/
Learn about the projects of the Monterey Bay Aquarium Research Institute in California.

INDEX